11/08

U.S. Sites and Symbols

★ ★ ★ ★ ★ ★ ★ ★ ★ ★ ★ ★

Galadriel Watson

WEIGL PUBLISHERS INC.

Published by Weigl Publishers Inc.
350 5th Avenue, Suite 3304, PMB 6G
New York, NY 10118-0069

Website: www.weigl.com

All of the Internet URLs given in the book were valid at the time of publication. However, due to the dynamic nature of the Internet, some addresses may have changed, or sites may have ceased to exist since publication. While the author and publisher regret any inconvenience this may cause readers, no responsibility for any such changes can be accepted by either the author or the publisher.

Library of Congress Cataloging-in-Publication Data

Watson, Galadriel Findlay.
 Trees/ Galadriel Watson.
          p.cm. – (U.S. sites and symbols)
 Includes index.
 ISBN: 978-1-59036-888-6 (hard cover: alk. Paper) – ISBN: 978-1-59036-889-3 (soft cover: alk. Paper) 1. State trees—United States—Juvenile literature. 2. State trees—United States—Pictorial works—Juvenile literature. I. Title.
QK85.W38 2009
582.160973—dc22

2008015829

Printed in the United States of America
1 2 3 4 5 6 7 8 9 0   12 11 10 09 08

Editor: Danielle LeClair
Designer: Kathryn Livingstone

Photograph Credits
Weigl acknowledges Shutterstock, iStockphoto, and Dreamstime as the primary image suppliers for this title. Unless otherwise noted, all images herein were obtained from Shutterstock, iStockphoto, Dreamstime, and their contributors.

Other photograph credits include: Alamy: pages 14 (top and bottom), 18 (bottom), 23 (bottom), 27 (top), 28 (middle), 30 (top), 36 (top front); Getty Images: pages 12 (top and bottom), 20 (top).

Every reasonable effort has been made to trace ownership and to obtain permission to reprint copyright material. The publishers would be pleased to have any errors or omissions brought to their attention so that they may be corrected in subsequent printings.

Contents

What are Symbols?

A symbol is an item that stands for something else. Objects, artworks, or living things all can be symbols. Every U.S. state has official symbols, or emblems. These items represent the people, history, and culture of the state. State symbols create feelings of pride and citizenship among the people who live there. Each of the 50 U.S. states has an official tree. It is called the state tree, or the arboreal emblem.

State Tree History

The first official state tree was chosen in 1907. Mrs. James C. Fessler decided her home state of Illinois should have an official tree and flower. She thought the best people to pick the tree and flower were the children of the state. In November of that year, schoolchildren in Illinois voted and chose the oak tree. It was named the state tree on July 1, 1908. Since that time, the state tree has been changed to the white oak. Soon, other states began to choose state trees. In 1919, Texas chose the pecan tree. Then, Indiana and Pennsylvania chose state trees in 1931.

The largest oak tree in the U.S. was the Wye Oak. When it fell, in 1953, it was 450 years old, and was 96 feet high.

Finding State Trees by Region

Alaska

Hawai'i

Washington

Montana

Oregon

Idaho

Wyoming

The West

Nevada

Utah

Colorado

California

Arizona

New Mexico

Each state has a tree symbol. In this book, the states are organized by region. These regions are the West, the Midwest, the South, and the Northeast. Each region is unique because of its land, people, and wildlife. Throughout this book, the regions are color coded. To find a state tree, first find the state using the map on this page. Then, turn to the pages that are the same color as that state.

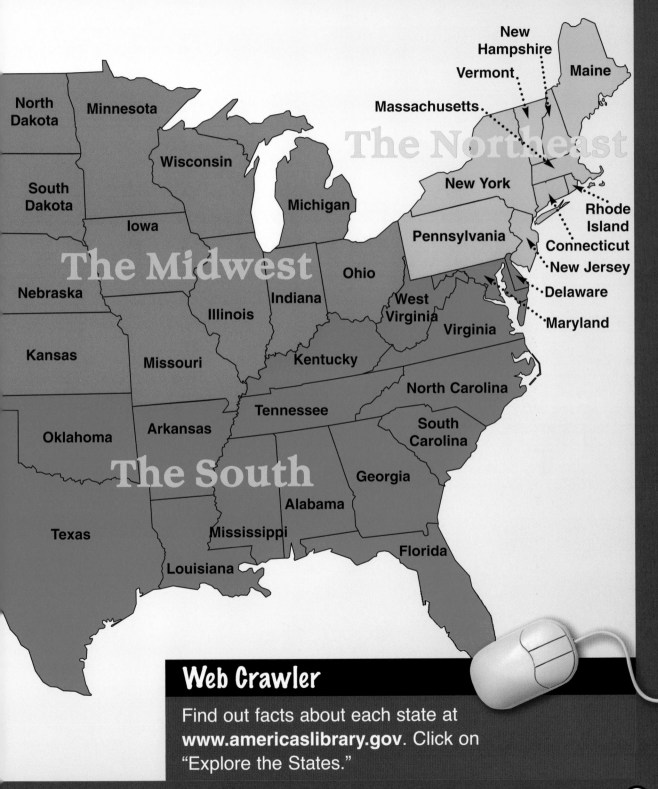

North Dakota

Minnesota

South Dakota

Wisconsin

Michigan

Iowa

Nebraska

Illinois

Indiana

Ohio

The Midwest

Kansas

Missouri

Kentucky

West Virginia

Virginia

Oklahoma

Arkansas

Tennessee

North Carolina

The South

South Carolina

Texas

Mississippi

Alabama

Georgia

Louisiana

Florida

The Northeast

New Hampshire

Vermont

Maine

Massachusetts

New York

Pennsylvania

Rhode Island

Connecticut

New Jersey

Delaware

Maryland

Web Crawler

Find out facts about each state at
www.americaslibrary.gov. Click on
"Explore the States."

The West

The West is made up of 13 states. They are Alaska, Arizona, California, Colorado, Hawai'i, Idaho, Montana, Nevada, New Mexico, Oregon, Utah, Washington, and Wyoming. Alaska is far to the north. It is separated from the rest of the country by Canada. The Pacific Ocean borders Alaska, Washington, Oregon, and California, and surrounds Hawai'i.

Colorado

Arizona

The West has many different landforms.
There are glaciers in Alaska and volcanoes on
Hawai'i. Giant redwood forests grow in Oregon.
Deserts cover parts of Arizona, California,
Nevada, and Utah. The Rocky Mountains run
through Alaska, Washington, Idaho, Montana,
Wyoming, Utah, Colorado, and New Mexico.

About 65 million people live in the West.
American Indians, Asians, Hispanics, and people
of British and German backgrounds make up the
largest cultural groups. Nearly four million
people live in Los Angeles, California. It is
the region's largest city.

Hawai'i

Alaska

Web Crawler

Trace important events in the
history of the West at **www.pbs.org/
weta/thewest/events**.

Discover the West's natural wonders by
clicking on the states at **www.nps.gov**.

California

Alaska
Sitka Spruce

The Sitka spruce became Alaska's state tree in 1962. It is the world's tallest species of spruce and can grow to be more than 200 feet tall. This spruce needs moist conditions to survive. It usually grows close to the ocean. For this reason, it is also called the tideland spruce or coast spruce. Its light, flexible wood has been used to make airplanes, ships, and musical instruments.

Arizona
Palo Verde

In Spanish, *palo verde* means "green stick." The tree was given this name because of its green trunk and branches. The palo verde lives in the desert of Arizona. It became the state tree in 1954. When there is a long drought, the leaves on the tree fall off. Its green bark contains **chlorophyll**. This helps the tree to keep **photosynthesizing**, even without leaves. In spring, the tree's bright yellow flowers make it a spectacular sight.

California
Coast Redwood & Giant Sequoia

California is home to two of the world's largest species of tree. They were adopted as the state trees in 1937. The coast redwood lives in mild, wet weather along the coast. The world's tallest tree species, it can reach more than 370 feet in height. The giant sequoia lives on the west side of the Sierra Nevada Mountains. It is shorter than the coast redwood but has a much larger trunk. Both species can live to be more than 2,000 years old.

Colorado
Colorado Blue Spruce

Often called the Colorado blue spruce, the blue spruce is native to the Rocky Mountains. It gets its name from its needles, which are silvery-blue. Sometimes called the silver spruce, it has short, stiff, sharp needles and long, thin cones. Colorado schoolchildren first picked the blue spruce to be the state tree in 1892. The choice became official in 1939.

Hawai'i
Candlenut Tree

The candlenut tree is the only state tree that is not native to its state. Originally from Malaysia and Polynesia, it was brought to Hawai'i about 1,500 years ago. The state chose it as its official tree in 1959. The tree gets its name from its nuts. They contain so much oil they can be lit like candles. The oil also is used to make varnish, soap, and paint. Locals call the tree *kukui*, which means "light" or "lamp."

Idaho
Western White Pine

The tallest white pine species in the world grows in Idaho. It measures 219 feet tall. Idaho chose the western white pine as its state tree in 1935. The tree's long, straight trunk is ideal for lumber. The tree's needles are blue-green with white lines. Cones can be up to 12 inches long.

Montana
Ponderosa Pine

Ponderosa pines are tall, straight trees. When young, their bark is nearly black. As the tree ages, the bark turns cinnamon-colored. When crushed, the tree's long needles smell of **turpentine** and citrus. Birds, such as great horned owls, live in ponderosa pines. The ponderosa pine is Montana's main lumber tree. It became the state tree in 1949.

Nevada
Singleleaf Pinyon Pine & Bristlecone Pine

Nevada's first state tree, chosen in 1959, was the singleleaf pinyon pine. This short, bushy tree grows in hot, dry areas. People eat its nuts. The bristlecone pine became the second state tree in 1987. This slow-growing pine lives in cold, dry conditions high on mountaintops. As it ages, it gets twisted and gnarled. It can live longer than almost any other thing on Earth. The oldest bristlecone pine was nearly 5,000 years old.

New Mexico
Pinyon Pine

The pinyon pine is best known for its edible seeds, called pine nuts. These seeds are hidden in deep pockets on the cones. People and wildlife enjoy the nuts. The pinyon pine grows in New Mexico's desert areas. It became the state tree in 1949.

Oregon
Douglas Fir

The Douglas fir is also known as the Oregon pine. The wood is said to be stronger than concrete. Oregon chose the Douglas fir as its state tree in 1939. The Douglas fir can grow to be more than 300 feet tall.

Utah
Blue Spruce

The pyramid-shaped, **symmetrical** blue spruce is sometimes used as a Christmas tree. It grows slowly and lives for a long time. The tree is fairly scarce. Its wood breaks easily and is full of knots, so it cannot be used for lumber. Utah chose the blue spruce for its state tree in 1933.

Washington
Western Hemlock

The western hemlock thrives in the humid conditions of the West Coast, as well as a moist belt on the west side of the Rocky Mountains. The tree's downward sweeping branches are covered with soft, flat needles and many small cones. Deer and elk feed off the tree. The western hemlock became Washington's state tree in 1947.

Wyoming
Plains Cottonwood

In 1947, Wyoming chose the plains cottonwood as the state tree. This tree can grow to be up to 100 feet tall, with a huge trunk and thick branches. It is a fast-growing tree, and its lifespan is only 70 years. Its leaves are triangular, and its seeds are fluffy. American Indians and early settlers used the tree to feed their horses and make items such as homes and canoes.

The Midwest

The Midwest is in the center of the United States. It lies between the Rocky Mountains in the west and the Appalachian Mountains in the northeast. The Ohio River separates the Midwest from the South. Canada lies to the north. There are 12 states in the Midwest. They are Illinois, Indiana, Iowa, Kansas, Michigan, Minnesota, Missouri, Nebraska, North Dakota, Ohio, South Dakota, and Wisconsin.

Ohio

South Dakota

Illinois

The area from North Dakota to Missouri is made up of mostly farming states. They are part of the **Great Plains**. The states from Minnesota to Ohio border the Great Lakes. This chain of freshwater lakes acts as a border between the United States and Canada.

Nearly 65 million people live in the Midwest. There are large groups of African Americans, American Indians, and people of European descent. Many people live in cities. Chicago is the largest city in the Midwest. It is home to three million people. Chicago and other Midwest cities are known for blues, jazz, rap, and rock.

Indiana

Web Crawler

Discover the wildlife of Illinois at
http://dnr.state.il.us/lands/education/kids/toc.htm.

Explore a virtual Midwest farmhouse at
www.pbs.org/ktca/farmhouses/vf.html.

Iowa

Illinois
White Oak

In 1908, schoolchildren chose the oak as the state tree of Illinois. Then, in 1973, schoolchildren voted again and chose the white oak. The white oak has

uniquely shaped leaves on wide, spreading branches. This makes it an excellent shade tree. It is called a white oak because its bark is a whitish color.

Indiana
Tulip Poplar

The border of Indiana's state seal shows a tulip poplar leaf. The tulip poplar has been the state tree since 1931. The tree's flowers look like tulips, giving it its name. The greenish-yellow flowers appear from April to June. They fall soon after blooming, leaving behind winged seeds, which spiral and fall slowly to the ground. This allows the seeds to scatter great distances. In 1923, the tulip poplar was also Indiana's state flower.

Iowa
Oak

Look in nearly any wooded area in Iowa and you will find its state tree, the oak. Thirteen species of oak grow in Iowa. The state chose the oak as its tree in 1961 because it is an important food source and shelter for birds and animals. The spreading tree produces lumber, used in items from tool handles to railroad ties.

Kansas
Cottonwood

If it looks like it is snowing in spring, it might not be snow, but the seeds falling from a cottonwood tree. The cottonwood is named for its fluffy, cottony seeds. It was chosen as the state tree in Kansas in 1937 because of its importance to settlers. There are few trees on the Prairies, so settlers used cottonwoods to build and heat their homes, cook meals, and as shade from the Sun in summer.

Michigan
Eastern White Pine

From 1870 to the early 1900s, most of the lumber in the United States was made in Michigan. Much

of this lumber came from the eastern white pine. This tree became the Michigan state tree in 1955. The tree has soft, flexible needles that range in color from bluish-green to silvery-green. Its curved cones are sticky to touch and smell strongly of pine.

Minnesota
Red Pine

The red pine is named for the tree's reddish-brown bark. They have long needles that snap when bent. Red pines can survive harsh weather and bad soils. Birds, such as bald eagles, nest in them. The red pine became Minnesota's state tree in 1945. The tallest red pine in Minnesota is 126 feet tall and more than 300 years old.

Missouri
Flowering Dogwood

The flowering dogwood is a beautiful tree that decorates the landscape. It became Missouri's state tree in 1955. In spring, tiny clusters of yellowish flowers stay in bloom for two to three weeks. These are surrounded by four large white or pink leaves. In the fall, the tree's leaves turn bright red, orange, or purple. Red berries dot the tree.

Nebraska
Cottonwood

In 1937, Nebraska's state tree was the American elm. In 1972, it changed to the cottonwood.

Cottonwoods have large, triangular leaves that turn yellow in fall. Settlers used the cottonwood as landmarks, and for lumber and fuel. Cottonwoods also pointed out sources of water to early settlers because they grow near rivers and streams.

North Dakota
American Elm

The American elm is the largest species of elm. It is a tall tree with drooping branches and leaves, and was once used to line streets. However, Dutch elm disease, introduced from Europe, killed many of these trees. This graceful tree is fast growing and can live to be up to 300 years old. North Dakota chose the American elm as its state tree in 1947.

Ohio
Buckeye

Ohio picked the buckeye to be its state tree in 1953. The buckeye is also called the horse chestnut. The tree got its name because the seed of a buckeye looks like the eye of a male deer, or buck. The seed is thought to be a good luck charm and can be eaten when cooked. Some people believe it can cure arthritis or headaches. Settlers carved utensils and wove baskets out of the tree's wood.

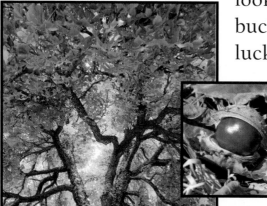

South Dakota
Black Hills Spruce

The forests surrounding South Dakota's Mount Rushmore are filled with Black Hills spruce. These trees are pyramid-shaped, with stiff, pointy needles and drooping cones. They are nice trees for yards, can survive bitter winters, and are sometimes used as Christmas trees. Their wood can be used for lumber. The Black Hills spruce became South Dakota's state tree in 1947.

Wisconsin
Sugar Maple

In 1893, children in Wisconsin chose the maple to be their state tree. Then, in 1949, after another vote, the sugar maple became the official state tree. The sap of the sugar maple makes the best maple syrup. The tree is known for its distinctively shaped leaves, seen on the Canadian flag, and its brilliant fall colors.

The South

The South is made up of 16 states. They are Alabama, Arkansas, Delaware, Florida, Georgia, Kentucky, Louisiana, Maryland, Mississippi, North Carolina, Oklahoma, South Carolina, Tennessee, Texas, Virginia, and West Virginia. The Atlantic Ocean borders the South from Delaware to the tip of Florida. A part of the Atlantic Ocean called the Gulf of Mexico stretches from Florida's west coast to Texas. Mexico lies to the south.

Trees

Florida

Alabama

Texas

The South is known for its warm weather. It also has plenty of rain. This makes it easy for plants to grow. In the past, cotton, tobacco, rice, and sugarcane were important crops in the South. They shaped southern history.

More than 100 million people live in the South. About 20 million are African American. Many people of Hispanic and European backgrounds also live there. Together, southerners share a special history and culture. Blues, gospel, rock, and country music all began in the South. Many well-known writers, such as Tennessee Williams, have lived there. The South is also known for its barbeque, Tex-Mex, and Cajun cooking.

West Virginia

Web Crawler

Read about the history of the South at **www.factmonster.com/ipka/A0875011.html**.

Explore the fun facts about the Southern states at **www.emints.org/ethemes/resources/S00000575.shtml**.

Mississippi

Alabama
Southern Longleaf Pine

The southern pine was first chosen as the state tree in 1949. Then, in 1997, the state tree was changed to the southern longleaf pine. This tree has very long needles that can grow up to 18 inches.

Arkansas
Pine

In 1939, Arkansas declared the pine to be its state tree. There are four types of pine trees in Arkansas. One of the most common is the loblolly pine. This tree's needles are about 6 to 9 inches long. Its cones are about the size of a potato.

Delaware
American Holly

American holly is most often used as a Christmas decoration. The tree's leaves are dark green and prickly. Only the female tree produces bright red berries. American holly was chosen as Delaware's state tree in 1939.

Florida
Cabbage Palmetto

The cabbage palmetto has no branches. Its long leaves extend right from the trunk. People eat its buds, called the "hearts of palm," though this kills the tree. The cabbage palmetto became the state tree of Florida in 1953. In 1970, it was added to the state seal.

Georgia
Live Oak

The live oak, also called the Virginia live oak, was chosen as the state tree of Georgia in 1937. It has oval, leathery leaves and acorns with bumpy, bowl-shaped caps. Settlers would use its long, arching branches to make the curved ribs of ships' hulls.

Kentucky
Tulip Poplar

The tulip poplar was first chosen as Kentucky's state tree in 1956. In 1973, it was found that this decision was never made official. The state chose the Kentucky coffee tree instead. However, in 1994, the tulip poplar was once again declared Kentucky's state tree.

Louisiana
Bald Cypress

Bald cypresses rise out of the swamps of Louisiana. They often have wide bases and "knees," or joints, that stick out of the water. These knees help the tree's roots get oxygen during floods. The tall, long-living bald cypress became Louisiana's state tree in 1963.

Maryland
White Oak

Oak trees are an important part of Maryland history. The Wye Oak was one of the oldest oaks in the United States, and the Richards White Oak was used as a landmark on a map from 1681. The white oak became Maryland's state tree in 1941.

Mississippi
Magnolia

After a vote by schoolchildren, the magnolia was named Mississippi's state tree in 1938. From May to June, this beautiful tree produces large, fragrant, white flowers.

North Carolina
Pine

North Carolina chose the pine to be its state tree in 1963. Early Americans used the pine to make resin, turpentine, and lumber for building ships. Its straight trunks still are used for lumber.

Oklahoma
Redbud

Early each spring, before the tree has grown leaves, the redbud bursts into flowers. These bright pink flowers come right out of the tree's twigs, branches, and trunk, making the redbud a spectacular sight. The flowers taste nutty and can be eaten in pancakes or salads. Redbud seed pods can be eaten, too. They are cooked and served like peas. In 1937, this beautiful tree became Oklahoma's state tree.

South Carolina
Cabbage Palmetto

South Carolina chose the cabbage palmetto, a palm tree, as its state tree in 1939. The tree also appears on the state flag and state seal. The cabbage palmetto grows farther north than any other palm tree. It can live in almost any soil, including sandy shores. The state chose the tree because, in 1776, a fort made of cabbage palmetto logs helped the people of South Carolina defend themselves against British invaders.

Tennessee
Tulip Poplar

The tulip poplar is neither a tulip nor a poplar. In fact, it is a member of the magnolia family. Tennessee chose the tulip poplar as its state tree in 1947. The tree grows quickly, can get very tall, and can live for 300 years. When one of its twigs is broken, it smells sweet and spicy.

Texas
Pecan

When the Texas governor died in 1906, a pecan tree was planted on his grave. In 1919, the people of Texas remembered this and chose the pecan to be their state tree. Pecans produce a nut that is eaten by both people and animals.

Virginia
Flowering Dogwood

Early American settlers made tea from the bark of the flowering dogwood to reduce fevers. These days, it is enjoyed for its beauty. The tree is small and blooms early in spring. In 1956, the flowering dogwood became the state tree of Virginia.

West Virginia
Sugar Maple

West Virginia named the sugar maple its state tree in 1949. Known for its sap, which is used to make maple syrup, the sugar maple provides excellent wood that can be used to make furniture.

The Northeast

The Northeast is the smallest region in the United States. It is east of the Great Lakes and south of Canada. The Atlantic Ocean borders the Northeast's east coast. There are nine states in the Northeast. They are Connecticut, Maine, Massachusetts, New Hampshire, New Jersey, New York, Pennsylvania, Rhode Island, and Vermont.

Connecticut

Vermont

Maine

New York

Many natural wonders are found in the Northeast. The Appalachian Mountains stretch through Maine, New Hampshire, Vermont, New York, and Pennsylvania. Lake Erie and Lake Ontario border New York. Niagara Falls flows between them. Half of Niagara Falls is located in the United States. The other half is located in Canada. On the U.S. side, the falls are 1,000 feet wide and 167 feet tall.

In the 1600s, the first settlers from Europe came to the area known as **New England**. Today, 55 million people live in the Northeast. More Irish Americans and Italian Americans live here than in any other part of the country. More than eight million people live in New York City, the largest city in the country.

Web Crawler

Learn more about New England at **www.discovernewengland.org**.

See spectacular views of Niagara Falls at **www.niagarafallsstatepark.com/Destination_ PhotoGallery.aspx**.

Pennsylvania

Connecticut
White Oak

One of the best-known trees in the United States was a white oak in Connecticut. In 1662, the king of England signed an important document giving rights to New England. In 1687, the next king wanted the document back. The people of New England kept it hidden inside an old, hollow white oak. To commemorate this, Connecticut chose the white oak as the state tree in 1947.

Maine
Eastern White Pine

The eastern white pine is the tallest tree species in the northeastern United States. Its tall, straight trunks were perfect for making ships' masts during colonial times. Today, the trunks are often used for telephone poles. These trees grow quickly, so they are also used for **reforestation** projects and landscaping.

Massachusetts
Mayflower

In 1775, George Washington took charge of the **Continental Army** while standing beneath an American elm in Massachusetts. In 1941, this tree became Massachusetts' state tree. The American elm is known for its beauty and its strong wood.

New Hampshire
White Birch

The white birch has white bark. This tree goes by many names. It is called the paper birch because its bark can be peeled and used as paper.

It is called the canoe birch because wide strips of its bark were once used to make canoes. This tree is found throughout New Hampshire. It became the state tree in 1947. In the fall, its leaves turn bright yellow.

New Jersey
Northern Red Oak

The beautiful red oak can be recognized by its pointy-lobed leaves with prickly tips. In fall, these leaves turn bright red. In 1950, the northern red oak became the state tree of New Jersey because of its beauty, strength, dignity, and long life. In the past, its acorns were an important food source for American Indians.

New York
Sugar Maple

Sugar maples grow in cool, moist climates. Unlike many other trees, they can grow in shady areas. Their winged seeds spin like helicopters as they fall from the tree. These trees can live for up to 400 years. They stop growing tall at about 150 years. After that, they only grow wider. New York was the fourth state to choose the sugar maple as its state tree, in 1956.

Pennsylvania
Eastern Hemlock

Settlers in early Pennsylvania used hemlock logs to build their cabins. Today, the hemlock is used to make paper. It was chosen as the state tree in 1931. It grows very slowly and can reach ages of 800 years or more.

Rhode Island
Red Maple

Rhode Island chose the red maple as its state tree in 1964. In winter, the stems of these trees turn red. In spring, its flowers are red. In summer, the tree's leaves attach to the stems on red stalks. In fall, its leaves turn red.

Vermont
Sugar Maple

The state of Vermont's official state tree is the sugar maple. It was chosen in 1949. The sap of the sugar maple is collected in late winter or early spring. One maple tree can produce about 20 gallons of syrup.

The National Arboreal Emblem

National emblems are symbols that are used for the entire country. The American flag, known as the star-spangled banner, is one such symbol. Another is the bald eagle, which is the national bird. The rose is the national flower. The official tree of the United States is the oak.

In 2004, Americans voted for the tree they thought should become the country's official tree. The oak won.

More than 60 types of oak tree grow in the United States. All oak trees start from acorns. Oaks grow up to 100 feet tall and can live for centuries.

Oaks have been important throughout American history. Their strong, thick wood has been used for ships' hulls and wine barrels.

History of the Oak

The oak tree has an important place in American history. Andrew Jackson was seen resting under an oak tree on his march to the Battle of New Orleans during the war of 1812. In addition, the naval ship, U.S.S. *Constitution*, launched in 1797, was given the nickname "Old Ironsides." It earned this name from the strength of its live oak hull, which became famous because it easily repelled British cannonballs.

Guide to State Trees

THE NATIONAL ARBOREAL EMBLEM
oak

ALABAMA
American longleaf pine

ALASKA
sitka spruce

ARIZONA
palo verde

ARKANSAS
pine

CALIFORNIA
coast redwood; giant sequoia

COLORADO
blue spruce

CONNECTICUT
white oak

DELAWARE
American holly

FLORIDA
cabbage palmetto

GEORGIA
live oak

HAWAI'I
candlenut

IDAHO
western white pine

ILLINOIS
white oak

INDIANA
tulip poplar

IOWA
oak

KANSAS
cottonwood

KENTUCKY
tulip poplar

LOUISIANA
bald cypress

MAINE
eastern white pine

MARYLAND
white oak

MASSACHUSETTS
American elm

MICHIGAN
eastern white pine

MINNESOTA
red pine

MISSISSIPPI
magnolia

MISSOURI
flowering dogwood

MONTANA
ponderosa pine

NEBRASKA
cottonwood

NEVADA
single leaf pinyon pine; bristlecone pine

NEW HAMPSHIRE
white birch

NEW JERSEY
northern red oak

NEW MEXICO
pinyon pine

NEW YORK
sugar maple

NORTH CAROLINA
pine

NORTH DAKOTA
American elm

OHIO
buckeye

OKLAHOMA
redbud

OREGON
douglas fir

PENNSYLVANIA
eastern hemlock

RHODE ISLAND
red maple

SOUTH CAROLINA
cabbage palmetto

SOUTH DAKOTA
Black Hills spruce

TENNESSEE
tulip poplar

TEXAS
pecan

UTAH
blue spruce

VERMONT
sugar maple

VIRGINIA
flowering dogwood

WASHINGTON
western hemlock

WEST VIRGINIA
sugar maple

WISCONSIN
sugar maple

WYOMING
plains cottonwood

Parts of the Tree

Trees are an important part of our daily lives. They provide shade and relief from the Sun, and they replenish our atmosphere with oxygen for us to breathe. Trees come in many different sizes, shapes, and colors. Still, they all share the same basic traits.

LEAVES AND NEEDLES Leaves and needles are a tree's food factory. Food-making, or photosynthesis, begins when the Sun's warmth and light are trapped by green chlorophyll in the leaves.

ROOTS The roots are an anchor, holding the tree in place. The roots grow and spread out underground from the root tips. They form a huge network that draws nutrients to the tree and protects the soil from **erosion**.

BUDS Each spring, a tree grows a new set of branches. Old branches grow taller and wider because they produce buds each spring.

CONES AND FLOWERS Trees produce flowers or cones that hold **fertilized** seeds. In late summer or fall, the seeds come loose and are scattered by wind, water, and wildlife.

TRUNK AND BRANCHES The trunk is the main stem of the tree. It supports the crown of branches and transports food and water throughout the tree. Branches and twigs support the leaves, holding them up to receive the Sun's light and warmth. They also produce buds that form new twigs, leaves, and flowers.

Test Your Knowledge

1 List the states that chose a spruce for the the state tree.

2 Name the tree that dies if you eat its "hearts of palm."

3 List the eleven state trees that are named after their colors.

4 Read the choices below. Which state pine tree smells of vanilla, turpentine, and citrus?
   a. western white pine
   b. pinyon pine
   c. ponderosa white pine
   d. southern longleaf pine
   e. bristlecone pine

5 What tree provides lumber that is stronger than concrete?

6 Which tree has fluffy seeds that fall from the it like snow?

7 Read the choices below. Which states each have two state trees?
   a. Alaska and Oregon
   b. Utah and Idaho
   c. Indiana and Rhode Island
   d. Calilfornia and Nevada

8 What is the national tree?

9 Read the trees below. Which tree has knees?
  a. pecan
  b. tulip poplar
  c. bald cypress
  d. sugar maple
  e. longleaf pine

12 What tree has nuts that can be lit like a candle?

13 Which state tree is most often used as a Christmas decoration?

10 What year was the first tree emblem chosen?

14 How many types of oak grow in the United States?

11 Read the trees below. Which tree can photosynthesize without leaves?
  a. blue spruce
  b. palo verde
  c. American Elm
  d. bald cypress
  e. red oak

15 Which tree is used to make paper?

Create Your Own Arboreal Emblem

Create a tree symbol to represent you. Begin by thinking about what type of tree you like. Use this book to help you. What kinds of trees grow in the region where you live? Will your tree be **coniferous** or **deciduous**?

Think about how your tree will look. Will your tree be large or small? Will it have leaves or needles? Will your tree grow flowers? Why? Look at the pictures in this book for help. You also can view more than 200 tree and shrub images at the Arbor Day Foundation site at **www.arborday.org/trees/treeguide/ browsetrees.cfm.**

Draw your tree on a piece of paper. Use the diagram on pages 42 and 43 to help you design the parts of your tree. Color your drawing with felt markers. When you are finished, label the parts of your tree.

Write a description of your tree. What kind of tree is it? Where does it grow? What does it say about you?

Further Research

Many books and websites provide information on state trees. To learn more about trees, borrow books from the library, or surf the Internet.

Books

Most libraries have computers that connect to a database for researching information. If you input a key word, you will be provided with a list of books in the library that contain information on that topic. Non-fiction books are arranged numerically, using their call number. Fiction books are organized alphabetically by the author's last name.

Websites

Find fun facts about each of the 50 U.S. states by clicking on this map from the U.S. Census Bureau. **www.census.gov/schools/facts**.

Learn about trees and forests at **http://ecokids.earthday.ca/pub/eco_info/topics/ forests/index.cfm**.

Read more about the regions of the United States at **www.factmonster.com/ipka/A0770177.html**.

Play online tree games and activities at **http://arborday.net/kids/teachingYouth.cfm**.

Glossary

chlorophyll: a substance in plants that captures light from the Sun

Continental Army: an army that formed in 1775, at the beginning of the American Revolutionary War with soldiers from all 13 of the original states

erosion: wearing away of Earth's surface by wind or water

fertilized: made capable of reproducing or of producing reproductive cells

Great Plains: a vast grassland region covering 10 U.S. states and 4 Canadian provinces. Used for farming and raising cattle

New England: the most northeastern U.S. states—Connecticut, Rhode Island, Massachusetts, New Hampshire, Vermont, and Maine

photosynthesizing: the way plants use sunlight to make food

reforestation: the act of planting trees to replace trees that have been cut down

symmetrical: close in size, shape, and position on both sides of something

turpentine: a mixture of oil and resin from certain pine trees, used as a paint thinner or to dissolve other substances

Index